CATERING SAFELY FOR FOOD ALLERGY SUFFERERS

A Chef's Guide

by
Michelle Berriedale-Johnson

Table of Contents

‖‖

Introduction

The regulations

The introduction of new regulations in December 2014, caused a seismic change in the UK's approach to catering for those with food allergies. No longer could eateries just brush off their food sensitive customers – 'Sorry, don't know – afraid we can't cater for you.' Every establishment, no matter how large or how small, now had to know whether any of their food contained any one of the 14 major allergens - as defined by EU law – and to be able to tell their customers about them.

The allergens are cereals containing gluten: wheat, barley, rye, oats; milk/dairy products; eggs; peanuts; lupin, [closely related to peanuts often cross reacts]; tree nuts; soya; sesame; fish; crustaceans; molluscs; celery and celeriac; mustard; sulphites at concentrations of more than 10 parts per million.

What the regulations meant

This did not mean, as many eateries interpreted it, that they had to provide allergen free food – nor did it mean that they had to print out all their menus with the allergens included. But what it did mean was that they, and their staff, had to know about any allergens in their food and had to be able to tell their customers about them, either in writing or verbally.

Initially, the implementation of the regulations caused chaos and many pronouncements of doom: all creative originality would be stifled; chefs would be de-skilled; eateries would go out of business....

The opportunity

As the industry got used to the idea, they realised that identifying any of the 14 major allergens in their food was not really that hard. Professional caterers now realised that there was a significant section of the eating out market (those with food allergies and intolerances) who, up until now, had just not eaten out. If they went a step further and offered menus and dishes that were allergen free, they could tempt those diners out into their establishments.

Gluten-free eating out and the growth of veganism

A whole new genre of dishes came into being: those that were either naturally or had been reworked to be free of gluten, to accommodate coeliac sufferers, and those who were trying to cut out, or at least lower, their consumption of gluten.

More adventurous eateries took the allergen-free idea further and also looked to exclude dairy products – a direction in which they were then jet-propelled by the recent explosion of interest in vegan eating.

Understanding how to do it

But although knowing about the 14 major allergens and even excluding them from your menus sounds easy, it is more complicated than it looks.

◎ Allergens in food are not always as easy to identify as they can go under many different names.

◎ Avoiding contamination of allergen-free food by allergen containing food requires organisation and discipline.

◎ Teaching staff to understand about allergens, and the sort of control that is needed – not to mention being able to deal empathetically with allergic or coeliac customers – requires time and patience.

◎ Although it is relatively easy to exclude some allergens from dishes, others may require a little time and creativity on the part of the chef to achieve a delicious offering.

This book

This manual is a shortcut to doing all those things.

1
What are food allergies and food intolerances?

It is estimated that between 5 per cent and 8 per cent of the population worldwide suffer from food allergies.

In medical terms, an allergy is an 'inappropriate response to a usually harmless substance' – in other words, the person with an allergy has an allergic reaction to something (it can be something they touch, something they breathe, something that stings them, or something they eat) that has no effect at all on those who do not suffer from allergy. This can vary from itching round the mouth, hives, swelling of the tongue and lips to full anaphylactic shock, from which a person could die.

What we are concerned with in this manual are those who react to foods that other people can eat without any problems at all. Below are different degrees of serious reactions.

SERIOUS, POTENTIALLY FATAL, FOOD ALLERGY

There are about 10 deaths per year from severe food allergy in the UK, the majority of which happen in a restaurant or when eating take-away food. These reactions can be caused by tiny amounts of the allergenic food – just a speck of peanut left on a serving spoon, for example.

The allergen can affect the whole body within minutes of eating or touching the food. The mouth and throat may swell up, making it difficult to breathe, while the blood pressure plummets so that the sufferer collapses and falls unconscious. This reaction is called anaphylaxis (pronounced anna-fill-axis). Unless Epinephrine (adrenaline), to counteract the drop in blood pressure, is administered within 10-15 minutes, the person can die. People who know they suffer from this condition always carry Epinephrine with them in the form of an auto-injector, better known by its brand name EpiPen. Other brands include Jext, Emerade and Auvi-Q.

The foods that most commonly cause anaphylaxis
- Peanuts: which are grown in the ground
- Tree nuts: walnuts, Brazil nuts, hazelnuts (also known as cobnut or filbert), almonds, cashew nuts, chestnuts, macadamia nuts, pecan nuts, hickory nuts
- Sesame seeds
- Shellfish
- Cow's milk products
- Eggs

FOOD INTOLERANCE

It is thought that between 20 per cent and 30 per cent of the population suffer from some degree of food intolerance at any one time.

An intolerance, or sensitivity to food, does not cause an immune system reaction and is not immediately life threatening but eating a food to which you are intolerant can make you very ill. Food intolerant people are not as sensitive as those who suffer serious food allergies, although some may still react to quite small quantities of their problem food.

Medical conditions which can cause you to react to certain foods include, among many others, irritable bowel syndrome (IBS), Crohn's disease, inflammatory bowel conditions, non-coeliac gluten intolerance, migraine, eczema, asthma, arthritis, anxiety and depression.

Cow's milk allergy

People who are cow's milk allergic will frequently be allergic to all other animal milks as the proteins are very similar. They must also exclude butter, ghee, cheese, including cottage cheese and cheese sauces, whey, cream, including sour cream, custard, buttermilk, powdered milk, evaporated milk, yoghurt and ice cream.

Cow's milk intolerance

People who are cow's milk intolerant may be able to tolerate other animal milks such as goat, sheep and buffalo, so might be able to have cream, butter, cheese or ice cream made from the milk of any of these animals.

Lactose intolerance

Lactose is a sugar found in all animal milks (including human). Lactose intolerance occurs when the individual does not make enough of the enzyme lactase to digest the lactose in the milk. There are now a number of lactose-free or lactose-reduced milks and milk products on the market, which most people with lactose intolerance can eat and drink successfully.

Coeliac disease

Strictly, coeliac disease is neither an allergy nor an intolerance. Instead, it is an autoimmune condition in which the villi (finger-like fronds in the small intestine that absorb nutrients) react to gliadin, a protein fraction (it is not a whole protein but a fraction of one) found in the gluten in wheat, and similar fractions found in the gluten in barley and rye. Eating gluten can make coeliac sufferers extremely ill and the only treatment for the disease is the full exclusion of gluten – which means a total avoidance of wheat, barley and rye. Some coeliac sufferers also react to oats. See Chapter 4.

FODMAPs intolerance

FODMAPs stands for Fermentable Oligo-, Di-, Mono-saccharides And Polyols – an umbrella name for a wide range of carbohydrates and sugars found in many foods. FODMAPs can ferment in the gut, or draw water into it, triggering a number of unpleasant digestive symptoms, such as bloating, diarrhoea and abdominal pain, principally in those with IBS.

Foods high in FODMAPs include:

◎ Wheat, onion, garlic, asparagus – the oligosaccharides fructans

◎ Fresh milk, cream – the disaccharide lactose

◎ Apples, mango, pears, corn syrups, honey – the monosaccharide fructose

◎ Cauliflower, mushrooms – the polyols

But not all FODMAP-intolerant people will be sensitive to all foods, or all categories.

Be guided by the customer.

Veganism

Vegans do not necessarily suffer from food allergy and intolerance but since they share a similar diet to people who are milk, dairy and/or egg allergic or intolerant, you may get vegans coming to your establishment if you offer milk-free or egg-free food.

Vegans do not eat any animal products or any animal derived products, so no eggs, no cheese, no animal milk yogurts, ice creams, butter, ghee, and no honey.

For explanations and definitions of some terms you may come across in discussions on allergy and intolerance, see our Glossary on page 54.

ORAL ALLERGY SYNDROME

Some people with a condition called oral allergy syndrome (OAS) react – usually mildly – to a number of raw fruits, vegetables, herbs and spices.

2
Intentional inclusion of allergens and accidental contamination with allergens

FOR AN ALLERGIC/INTOLERANT PERSON OR A COELIAC,
THERE ARE TWO DANGERS:

THE ALLERGEN AS AN INGREDIENT

If a food allergic person is shopping in a supermarket, they can check the ingredients in everything they buy by reading the ingredients list on the label. As long as they know all the names under which their allergen may be listed they will be able to avoid that ingredient by not buying the product.

In a restaurant, café, snack bar or canteen, there is rarely a list of ingredients to guide them. However, under the regulations that came into force in December 2014, any outlet selling food must:

1 Know whether any of the 14 major allergens are in any of the foods they are selling.

2 Be able to tell their customer which allergens are in which foods. This can be done verbally by serving staff/chefs, or they can offer the customer written details.

3 Display a sign telling the customer that they can provide information about any allergens in the food.

Most deaths from allergy in catered situations have occurred when the allergens were deliberately included in the dish, but the allergic person did not realise because:

◎ they did not expect them to be there, they were an unusual ingredient in that dish – peanuts in a pesto sauce for example, or,

◎ because they were wrongly informed by the staff who did not know themselves that the dish was free of the ingredient in question when in fact it was not.

It is therefore vitally important that at least one person is always available in any catering outlet who understands about allergy and knows which allergens are used in which dishes.

14 MAJOR ALLERGENS *

ALLERGEN	WHAT TO LOOK FOR ON THE LABEL
1: Celery This includes celery stalks, leaves, seeds and the root. Usually found in celery salt, salads, some meat products, soups and stock cubes.	Celery seed, Celery leaf, Celery salt, Celeriac or Celariac, Celery stalk and products made from celery.
2: Cereals Wheat, rye, barley and oats are often found in foods containing flour, some baking powder, batter, breadcrumbs, cakes, couscous, meat products, pasta, pastry, sauces, soups and some fried food.	Wheat, Durum wheat, Semolina, Spelt, Kamut (from Khorasan wheat), Eincorn, Faro, Barley, Rye, Oat, Malt, Couscous and products made from wheat.
3: Crustaceans Crabs, lobster, prawns and scampi are crustaceans. Shrimp paste is an allergen in this category that is commonly used in Thai and Southeast Asian cooking.	Amphipods, Barnacles, Crabs, Hermit Crabs, Crayfish, Isopods, Lobsters, Mantis Shrimp, Mussel Shrimp, Mysids, Sea Spiders, Shrimp, Prawns and products made with crustaceans.
4: Eggs Eggs are found in cakes, some meat products, mayonnaise, mousses, pasta, quiche, sauces and pastries. Some food products are glazed with eggs during cooking.	Albumin, Apovitellin, Cholesterol free egg substitute, Dried egg solids, Dried egg, Egg, Egg white, Egg yolk, Egg wash, Eggnog, Fat substitutes, Globulin, Livetin, Lysozyme, Mayonnaise, Meringue, Meringue powder, Ovalbumin, Ovoglobulin, Ovomucin, Ovomucoid, Ovotransferrin, Ovovitelia, Ovovitellin, Powdered eggs, Silici albuminate, Simplesse, Surimi, Trailblazer, Vitellin, Whole egg and products made with egg.

ALLERGEN	WHAT TO LOOK FOR ON THE LABEL
5: Fish You may find fish sauces in pizzas, relishes, salad dressings, stock cubes and Worcestershire sauce.	Anchovies, Bass, Catfish, Cod, Flounder, Grouper, Haddock, Hake, Halibut, Herring, Mahi Mahi, Perch, Pike, Pollock, Salmon, Scrod, Swordfish, Sole, Snapper, Tilapia, Trout, Tuna and products made with fish.
6: Lupin Lupin is a flower, but it is also sometimes found in flour and is most commonly used in bread, pastries and pasta.	Lupine, Lupin flour, Lupin seed, Lupin bean and any products made from lupin.
7: Molluscs Includes mussels, land snails, squid and whelks, but can also be found in oyster sauce, which is commonly used in fish stews for example.	Abalone, Clams, Cockles, Mussels, Octopus, Oysters, Scallops, Snails, Squid and any products made from Molluscs.
8: Mustard This includes Mustard in the form of powder, liquid and seeds. This ingredient is used in breads, curries, marinades, meat products, salad dressings, sauces and soups.	Mustard powder, Mustard seeds, Mustard flour, Mustard leaves, Mustard oil, Sprouted mustard seeds and any products made from mustard.

*The most up-to-date list at the time of publishing.
The website erudus.com also has industry updates.

9: MILK

ALLERGEN: Milk is found in dairy products such as butter, cheese, cream, milk powders and yoghurt. Some foods are also glazed with milk during cooking. It's also commonly found in powdered soups and sauces.

What to look for on the label

Milk – acidophilus milk, buttermilk, buttermilk blend, buttermilk solids, cultured milk, condensed milk, dried milk, dry milk solids (DMS), evaporated milk, fat free milk, full cream milk powder, goat's milk, lactose free milk, low fat milk, malted milk, milk derivative, milk powder, milk protein, milk solids, milk solid pastes, nonfat dry milk, nonfat milk, nonfat milk solids, pasteurised milk, powdered milk, sheep's milk, skim milk, skim milk powder, sour milk, sour milk solids, sweet cream buttermilk powder, sweetened condensed milk, sweetened condensed skim milk,whole milk, 1% milk, 2% milk.

Butter – artificial butter, artificial butter flavour, butter, butter extract, butter fat, butter flavoured oil, butter solids, dairy butter, natural butter, natural butter flavour, whipped butter.

Casein and caseinates – ammonium caseinate, calcium caseinate, hydrolyzed casein, iron caseinate magnesium caseinate, potassium caseinate, sodium caseinate, zinc caseinate.

Cheese – cheese (all types), cheese flavor (artificial and natural), cheese food, cottage cheese, cream cheese, imitation cheese, vegetarian cheeses with casein

Cream - Whipped cream, Curds, Custard, Dairy product solids, Galactose, Ghee, Half & Half Hydrolysates – Casein hydrolysate, Milk protein hydrolysate, Protein hydrolysate, Whey hydrolysate, Whey protein hydrolysate Ice cream, Ice milk, Sherbet, Casein, Whey, Lactoalbumin, Lactulose, Lactoferrin, Lactoglobulin, Milk protein, Hydrolysate, Lactalbumin, Lactalbumin phosphate, Lactate solids, Lactyc yeast, Lactitol monohydrate, Lactoglobulin, Lactose, Lactulose, Milk fat, anhydrous milk fat, Nisin preparation, Nougat, Pudding, Quark, Recaldent, Rennet, Rennet casein, Simplesse® (fat replacer), Sour cream, Sour cream solids, Imitation sour cream, Whey – acid whey, Cured whey, Delactosed whey, Demineralised whey, Hydrolyzed whey, Powdered whey, Reduced mineral whey, Sweet dairy whey, Whey, Whey protein, Whey protein concentrate, Whey powder, Whey solids, Yogurt (regular or frozen), Yogurt powder and any products made from milk.

10: NUTS

ALLERGEN: Nuts (tree nuts) (excluding Peanuts) refers to nuts that are grown on trees; unlike peanuts, which are grown in the ground. This includes all tree nuts like cashew nuts, almonds and hazelnuts.

WHAT TO LOOK FOR ON THE LABEL

Almond, Hazelnuts, Walnuts, Cashews, Pecan Nuts, Brazil Nuts, Pistachio Nuts, Macadamia or Queensland Nuts.

DETAILED LIST:

Almond, Almond paste, Anacardium nuts, Anacardium occidentale (Anacardiaceae) [botanical name, Cashew], Bertholletia excelsa (Lecythidaceae) [botanical name, Brazil nut], Carya illinoensis (Juglandaceae) [botanical name, Pecan], Cashew, Castanea pumila (Fagaceae) [botanical name, Chinquapin], Hazelnut, Juglans spp. (Juglandaceae) [botanical name, Walnut, Butternut, Heartnut] Karite (shea nut), Lichee nut, Litchi chinensis Sonn. Sapindaceae [botanical name, Lichee nut] Lychee nut, Macadamia nut, Macadamia spp. (Proteaceae) [botanical name, Macadamia nut/Bush nut], Mandelonas, Marzipan, Mashuga nuts, Nangai nuts, Natural nut extract (for example, almond extract), Nougat, Nu-Nuts®, Nut butters (e.g., Almond butter, Hazelnut butter, Brazil nut butter, Macadamia nut butter, Pistachio nut butter, Shea nut butter, Karike butter, as well as other nut butters), Nut meal, Nutella ®, Nutmeat, Nut oil (e.g., Walnut oil as well as other nut oils), Nut paste, Nut pieces, Pecan, Pignolia, Pili nut, Pine nut, Pine nut (Indian, piñon, pinyon, pigndi, pigñolia, pignon nuts), Pinon nut, Piñon or Piñon nut, Pinus spp. (Pineaceae) [botanical name, Pine nut/piñon nut], Pistachio, Pistacia vera L. (Anacardiaceae) [botanical name, Pistachio], Pralines, Prunus dulcis (Rosaceae) [botanical name, almond] Shea nut, Sheanut, Vitellaria paradoxa C.F. Gaertn. (Sapotaceae) [botanical name, Shea nut] Walnut (English, Persian, Black, Japanese, California) and any products made with nuts.

ALLERGEN	WHAT TO LOOK FOR ON THE LABEL
11: Peanuts Often used as an ingredient in biscuits, cakes, curries, desserts, sauces, groundnut oil and peanut flour.	Ground Nuts, Beer nuts, Monkey nuts, Nut meat, Arachis oil, Kernels, Peanut protein, Arachic oil, Arachis, Arachis hypogaea, Artificial nuts, Boiled peanuts, Cold pressed, Extruded or expelled peanut oil, Crushed nuts, Crushed peanuts, Earth nuts, Goober peas, Ground nuts, Ground peanuts, Hydrolyzed peanut protein, Mandelonas, Mixed nuts, Nut pieces, Nutmeat, Peanut butter, Peanut butter chips, Peanut butter morsels, Peanut flour, Peanut paste, Peanut sauce, Peanut syrup, Virginia peanuts and any products made with peanuts.
12: Sesame & sesame seeds These are found commonly in bread, usually sprinkled on buns such as hamburger buns, bread sticks, hummus, sesame oil and tahini.	Sesame seeds, Sesame oil, Benne, Benne seed, Gingelly, Gingelly oil and any products made with sesame.

ALLERGEN	WHAT TO LOOK FOR ON THE LABEL
13: Soya Found sometimes in bean curd, edamame beans, miso paste, textured soya protein, soya flour or tofu, soya is a staple ingredient in oriental food. It can be found in desserts, ice cream, meat products, sauces and vegetarian products.	Soy flour, Soya Milk, Soya nuts, Bean curd, Edamame (soybeans in pods), Hydrolyzed soy protein, Kinnoko flour, Kyodofu (freeze dried tofu), Miso, Natto, Okara (soy pulp), Shoyu sauce, Soy albumin, Soy concentrate, Soy fiber, Soy formula, Soy grits, Soy milk, Soy miso, Soy nuts, Soy nut butter, Soy protein, Soy protein concentrate, Soy protein isolate, Soy sauce, Soy sprouts, Soya, Soya flour, Soybeans, Soybean granules, Soybean curd, Soybean flour, Soy lecithin, Soybean paste, Supro, Tamari, Tempeh, Teriyaki sauce, Textured soy flour (TSF), Textured soy protein (TSP), Textured vegetable protein (TVP), Tofu, Yakidofu, Yuba (bean curd), Soy oil, Soybean, Textured vegetable protein, Edemame, Bean curd, Vegetable starch, Vegetable gum and any products containing soya.
14: Sulphur Dioxide (sulphites) This is an ingredient often used in dried fruits and in some meat products, soft drinks, vegetables, wine and beer. Asthmatics have a higher risk of developing an allergy to sulphites.	Sulphur, Sulphur Dioxide, Sulphite, Sulphites, Potassium bisulphite, Metabisulphite, Sodium bisulphite, Dithionite, Metabisulphite, Sulphiting agents, Sulphurous acid, E220 Sulphur dioxide, E221 Sodium sulphite, E222 Sodium hydrogen sulphite, E223 Sodium metabisulphite, E224 Potassium metabisulphite, E226 Calcium sulphite, E227 Calcium hydrogen sulphite, E228 Potassium hydrogen sulphite, E150b Caustic sulphite caramel, E150d Sulphite ammonia caramel and any products containing sulphur dioxide (sulphites).

For more about these allergens and the products they can be found in, see Chapter 4.

ACCIDENTAL CONTAMINATION

In a busy kitchen or restaurant, the risk that non-allergenic foods will get contaminated by potentially allergenic foods is high.

For example, if someone is filling a dish with peanuts, it is easy to get peanut dust on their hands, which could then be transferred to a different dish in which peanuts are not an ingredient.

Or, if the same serving spoon is used both to serve vegetables in a creamy sauce and vegetables to someone who cannot eat dairy products, the cream on the spoon may be transferred to the milk-product-free vegetables.

You can see that it is therefore vitally important that food, which is to be served to an allergic customer, is prepared by someone who is aware of the possible dangers and prepared with utensils free of allergens. They must take every precaution to avoid contamination by washing their hands thoroughly, before working with the allergen-free ingredients, ensuring that the allergen-free ingredients never come into contact with allergens, and by only using implements and dishes which they are sure have been washed thoroughly. Ideally, there should be separate equipment for use only with allergy free products.

In Chapter 5, we go into this in more detail.

3
The law and your liabilities

Since December 13th 2014, information on any of the 14 allergens used as ingredients must be provided for ALL foods sold through the food service industry whether in a works canteen, a five-star restaurant, a hospital, a school, a café, a snack bar or a stand at a football ground.

This information can be printed, written down on a chalk board or chart, or provided orally by a member of staff. Where the specific allergen information is not obviously visible, a clear sign must be provided to where this information can be obtained.

These rules will only cover information about major allergens intentionally used as ingredients. They do not cover allergens present following accidental contact e.g. contamination. It depends on whether you have shown 'due diligence' in your food preparation as to whether this contamination would have been avoidable.

Article 79 of the EU Food Information for Consumers Regulation No. 1169/2011 regulations states that:

Allergen information for non-prepacked food can be communicated through a variety of means to suit the business format of the FBO [food business outlet]. The requirement is to provide information about the use of allergenic ingredients in a food. The provision does not require food businesses to provide a full ingredients list. Where food business [sic] choose for this information to not be provided upfront in a written format (for example allergen information on the menu), the food business should use clear signposting to direct the customer to where this information can be found, such as asking members of staff. In such situations there must be a statement that can be found on food menus, chalkboards, food order tickets, food labels or webpages (see Regulation 5 (4) of the Food Information Regulations 2014).

NB: As of 2021, the regulations will change to require foods known as 'prepacked for direct sale' – such as sandwiches which have been made earlier in the day and placed on a shelf for sale – to carry full ingredient listings.

In this context 'allergenic ingredients' refers to any of the 14 major allergens.

Enforcement of these regulations lies with both Environmental Health officers and Trading Standards officers.

Failure to comply with the regulations is a criminal offence and may result in a criminal prosecution and a fine of £5,000. Prosecutions are made under the personal injury act. If a person dies as a result of a food outlet's negligence, owners and staff can be convicted of manslaughter, or unlawful killing by reason of gross negligence. The sentence is a maximum of 18 years.

NB: While the regulations do require you to know about the allergens in your foods, they do NOT require you to provide your customers with 'free-from' foods (foods free of allergens) – that is entirely at your discretion. However, many food service operators have found that offering 'free-from' foods is both relatively simple and very rewarding.

Other legal protections for allergic consumers

Allergic people are also protected under existing food and consumer protection laws.

The Food Safety Act 1990 and the Food Safety Regulations 1995 (revised from 1st January 2006) require caterers to provide 'safe' food to their customers. Safe food includes allergen-free food if you have specifically been asked to provide allergen-free food.

A customer suffering an adverse reaction to a caterer's product may also sue for compensation, under the Consumer Protection Act 1987, as a result of being sold a 'defective' product.

A product could be considered 'defective in respect of information' if the presence of an allergen of which the caterer was, or should have been, aware was not made clear to a customer or if it contained even a tiny amount of an allergen which should not have been there.

However, the caterer may be able to refute charges of negligence if they can show that they have operated according to Due Diligence procedures. This requires suitable training of staff as to the risks, and how to respond. They would still be 'negligent in respect of information' if they should have been aware of a significant risk of cross contamination and did not inform the allergic customer.

'May Contain': precautionary allergen labelling (accidental contamination)

The regulations do not cover any accidental allergen contamination, although under the Food Safety Action and the Consumer Protection Acts, (see above) an allergic consumer would still have legal protection provided they had told the establishment about their allergy.

The Food Standards Agency (FSA) recommends that: 'Advisory labelling on possible cross-contamination with allergens should be justifiable only on the basis of a risk assessment applied to a responsibly managed operation. Warning labels should only be used where there is a demonstrable and significant risk of allergen cross-contamination, and they should not be used as a substitute for Good Manufacturing Practices.'

In other words, provided you have taken all possible precautions to avoid cross contamination and are confident that you have done so safely, you should not use 'may contain' warnings. However, if you genuinely believe that there is a risk, then you should explain that risk to your customer so that they can make an 'informed decision' as to whether or not they wish to eat the food.

If an ingredient that you use (a sauce or a stock, for example) carries a 'may contain' warning, you should tell your customer that this is the case so that they can decide whether they should eat it.

4
Danger foods: the major allergens

The foods that you need to concern yourself with in the first instance are the 14 major allergens as these are the ones that you are required, by law, to know about. However, there are a number of other quite common foods and ingredients to which people may react, so we have included a few of those as well.

Most of these foods are known by several different names but, under the new regulations, the allergen should always be highlighted on the lists of ingredients in pre-packed foods, typically in bold, but possibly in capitals or underlined, and within brackets if found in a compound ingredient. For example: "barley malt vinegar" or "mayonnaise (vegetable oil, EGG, lemon juice)".

However, if the ingredients have not been properly labelled, perhaps because they come from outside the EU, they may not appear like this – or appear at all.

If you are in any doubt, leave the ingredient out!

Remember, that for someone with a serious allergy to a particular food, even the tiniest amount can be enough to cause a reaction, so it is really important to check all the ingredients.

See below for allergens and what they are used in.

CEREALS CONTAINING GLUTEN (WHEAT*, RYE, BARLEY AND OATS**)

Wheat is also known as:
Bran
Bulgar
Cereal Binder/Filler
Chilton/Dinkel
Couscous
Durum Wheat
Edible/Food Starch
Einkorn/Farro
Emmer/Triticum/Triticale
Flour (plain, self-raising, wholemeal, malted, bread)
Graham Flour
Kamut/Khorasan/Spelt *
Modified Starch
Rusk
Semolina
Wheatgerm
Wheat Starch

NB. Buckwheat, although it has 'wheat' in the name, is not a wheat. Barring any cross-contamination issues, buckwheat is safe for coeliac sufferers and for those with a wheat allergy or intolerance.

* Spelt, Khorasan wheat or kamut

Artisan, craft and health food bakeries are now using varieties of 'old' wheats such as spelt, Khorasan and kamut. They are thought to be healthier and some people who have difficulty digesting modern, industrially baked breads find them easier to digest. However, they are still wheat so should NOT be served to anyone with coeliac disease or a wheat allergy.

** Oats

Although oats are listed as a 'cereal containing gluten' the type of gluten they contain is slightly different to that in wheat, barely and rye and is not thought to be harmful for most coeliac sufferers in modest quantities. However, because oats and wheat are often grown or milled very close together there is always a high risk of contamination so you should only use oats which are certified as being gluten free, i.e. have not been grown near, or milled with, wheat.

Barley is also known as:
Barley malt
Cereal fibre
Dietary fibre
Hordeum
Malt d'orge

NB: **Maltodextrin**. Although it looks as though it may contain malt/barley, it does not, and is safe for coeliac sufferers.

Rye is also known as:
Secale cereale

WHERE CAN YOU FIND THEM?

They are likely to be found in any processed or manufactured food so do check labels carefully for bread, baked goods, baking mixes, pasta, crackers, cereals, condiments, chocolates, sauces.

Because wheat, barley and rye are major allergens they should always appear in bold (possibly in brackets) after any ingredient of which they are a constituent part or are derived from one of the grains – for example "modified starch (**wheat**)".

NB: The word 'gluten' may not appear in the ingredients, so look for the name of the cereal containing gluten.

SOME UNEXPECTED PLACES IN WHICH YOU MIGHT FIND WHEAT, BARLEY OR RYE:

Baking powder
Beer (both barley and wheat)
Bottled sauces of all kinds, including horseradish
Cereal binder/filler/protein and/or rusk
Cheese spread/dips and taramasalata
Curry powders
Monosodium Glutamate (MSG)
Salad dressings
Sausages
Textured vegetable/vegetable protein (this can be from other sources)
Whisky (barley and rye) – although this is a distilled spirit, so no proteins should be left although very sensitive coeliac sufferers may still react or avoid.

MILK AND MILK PRODUCTS

Remember that 'milk products' include not only milk but cream, butter, cheese, yogurt and ice cream – but NOT eggs.

Is also known as:
Buttermilk
Casein/Caseinates
Crème Fraîche
Fromage Frais
Ghee
Hydrolysed Casein/Whey
Lactose
Whey
Whey Protein/Sugar

WHERE CAN YOU FIND THEM?

Milk products are found in many processed, manufactured and baked foods so do check labels carefully.

For some milk-based ingredients – yogurt, butter, cream – just that word may be highlighted, without the presence of the word 'milk' – so you need to be vigilant.

Alternatively, the word 'milk' may appear (possibly in brackets) after any ingredient derived from milk – for instance "Quark (milk)".

SOME UNEXPECTED PLACES IN WHICH YOU MIGHT FIND MILK OR MILK PRODUCTS:

Animal fat
Artificial cream
Batter (for chicken, pancakes, waffles, fish fingers, fish, sausages, onion rings, tempura, bhaji, donuts, churros)
Breads – many enriched breads will include butter and/or milk
Cheese straws/biscuits and cheese flavoured crisps
Chocolate/chocolate products
Low fat spreads and margarine
Sweeteners
Vegetable fats

EGGS

Are also known as –
Albumin
Apovitellin
Globulin
Livetin
Lysozyme
Ovalbumin
Ovoglobulin
Ovomucin
Ovomucoid
Ovotransferrin
Ovovitelia
Ovovitellin
Silici albuminate

WHERE CAN YOU FIND THEM?

Eggs are used in many processed, manufactured and baked foods so do check labels carefully.

SOME UNEXPECTED PLACES IN WHICH YOU MIGHT FIND EGG OR EGG PRODUCTS:

The alcoholic drink Advocaat
Batter on deep fried food
Brioche and other enriched bread
Egg noodles and some pasta
Glazes on desserts or baked goods
Ice cream
Marzipan

PEANUTS

Can also be known as:
Arachide
Arachis oil
Beer Nuts
Cacahuete
Earth nuts
Goober Nuts/Peas
Groundnuts
Mandalona nuts
Monkey nuts

Peanuts are used as an ingredient in peanut butter and some processed/manufactured foods (such as satay sauce) although not in very many. However, they can also be used as a substitute for more expensive ingredients such as ground almonds, so do be sure to check labels very carefully.

SOME UNEXPECTED PLACES IN WHICH YOU MIGHT FIND PEANUT OR PEANUT PRODUCTS:

Almond powder and chopped almonds can contain peanuts
Bakery products sold loose can pick up traces of peanut
Chinese and Indonesian dishes in general
Chocolate from Poland
Curry sauce
Hydrolysed vegetable protein (occasionally)
Oil in which peanut products have previously been fried
Sweets like nougat and marzipan

LUPIN

It now seems clear that lupin can cross react with peanuts so anyone with a peanut allergy may also react to lupin flour.

WHERE CAN YOU FIND IT?

Lupin is used mainly in baked goods, especially on the continent, and sometimes in gluten-free pastas and in pastry cases, pies, waffles, pancakes, crêpes, products containing crumb, pizzas, vegetarian meat substitute, batter-coated vegetables such as onion rings.

TREE NUTS

These are almond, Brazil nut, cashew, hazelnut, macadamia, pecan, pistachio and walnut.

NB: Nutmeg, coconut, chufa (tiger) nuts and pine nuts are NOT 'tree nuts' and do not normally trigger allergic reactions.

Allergic reactions to chestnuts – also not listed as tree nuts in the legislation – are rare and usually only affect the lips and mouth (OAS).

WHERE CAN YOU FIND THEM?

All Greek/Arabic desserts
Breads, biscuits, cake and many baked goods
Chocolate and confectionery
Marzipan
Some vegetarian dishes/ready meals

SESAME SEEDS

Also known as:
Anjoli
Benniseed/Benne
Cingili/Gingelly
Gomashio
Halva
Hummus and tahini
Sim-sim
Teel/Till

Anything bought from a deli where sesame is used
All breads made in a bakery where sesame is used
All Chinese, Indonesian, Japanese, Greek, Mexican and Lebanese food
Many crackers, buns, bagels and rice cakes
Health, energy and snack bars
Vegetarian dishes and ready meals

NB: Sesame oil is rarely refined, so is allergenic

SOYBEANS

Are also known as:
Edamame
Miso
Natto
Cold Pressed Soya Oil
Tempeh
Tofu
Textured Vegetable Protein/Vegetable Protein (this can also be made from corn, but should be declared as soya if it is soya)

Almost any manufactured food – as soya flour or oil.
Chinese, Japanese and Far Eastern foods
Emulsifiers
Lecithin in chocolate (although lecithin can also be made from sunflower seeds and egg yolk)
Teriyaki sauce
Vegetable protein, starch and shortening (these can also be corn based)

NB: Soya is widely used in animal feed and those who are super-sensitive may be unable to eat meat that have been fed on soya.

CELERY AND CELERIAC

Can also be known as:
Celariac
Celeriac root
Celery salt

WHERE CAN YOU FIND IT?

Any homemade stock as it is a base ingredient
Any ready prepared meals, fresh or frozen, especially vegetarian ones
Bouillon/stock cubes
Marmite
Salads
Salad dressings
Sandwiches
Spice mixes

MUSTARD

Can also be known as:
Moutarde
Mustard greens
Mustard seed

WHERE CAN YOU FIND IT?

Mayonnaise
Ready meals and soups of any kind, fresh or frozen
Salad dressings
Sauces
Spice mixes of any kind

SULPHUR DIOXIDE OR SULPHITES

Allergy to sulphites is rare, although 3 per cent to 10 per cent of the asthmatic population are sulphite sensitive.

There are a large number of foods that contain naturally occurring sulphites, but sulphur dioxide is also very widely used in the food and drink industry mainly as a preservative.

They can be known as:
Potassium metabisulphite
Sodium bisulphite
Sodium sulphite
Sulfur dioxide

Sulphur dioxide exists naturally in all foods, all food contains some level of sulphur dioxide. The following foods often contain high levels of added sulphites for preservation purposes and those who are sensitive to sulphites will want to avoid them:

Fish: crustaceans (shellfish)
Some fresh fruits and vegetables
Dried fruits and vegetables
Jams, jellies, marmalades (sulphite is in the pectin)
Mincemeat, pickles and relishes
Sweeteners: glucose solids and syrup
Tomato paste, pulp, ketchup, purée

FISH, CRUSTACEANS AND MOLLUSCS

People can be allergic just to crustaceans (barnacles, crab, crayfish, krill, lobster, prawns or all types, shrimp) or to molluscs (abalone, clams, cockles, cuttlefish, limpets, mussels, octopus, oyster, scallop, slugs, snails, squid) or to any freshwater or seawater fish. Those who are sensitive can be very sensitive, to the point that they will react even to inhaled fish cooking vapour.

SOME UNEXPECTED PLACES IN WHICH YOU MIGHT FIND CRUSTACEANS OR MOLLUSCS?

Aspic
Caviar of all kinds
Isinglass
Many spicy southeast Asian sauces
Worcestershire sauce

Be aware that because they are not major allergens, they do not have to be declared as such so will not be highlighted on the ingredients list. Neither will they be listed if they are a part of a composite ingredient such as vegetable starch. It may be difficult to find out exactly what the base is.

Corn/maize

Although corn is not one of the 14 major allergens, corn allergy is relatively common, especially in North America. Corn/maize is a widely used ingredient in processed and manufactured food, especially in 'free-from' food as it is the most commonly used substitute for wheat, so it is a particularly hard allergy to live with.

Can also be known as:
Cereal Starch
Corn on the Cob/Sweetcorn
Cornmeal
Corn Starch
Corn Syrup/High Fructose Corn Syrup (HFCS)
Dextrose and Glucose Syrup
Edible/Food starch
Malt/Flavouring
Modified starch
Polenta
Thickener
Vegetable Gum, Oil and Starch

WHERE WILL YOU FIND IT?

All processed, manufactured or baked goods, especially 'free-from' ones as corn is the most common substitute for wheat.
All 'mixes' for products like gravy, desserts sauces
Baking powder
Chewing gum and sweets
Cured meats
Dextrose and glucose syrup
Hot chocolate
Ice cream
Sweetened iced teas
Icing sugar and salt (used to make it run smoothly)
Juice drinks and Juices with preservatives (even if they claim to be 100 per cent juice)
Margarine
Medicines and supplements (used as a filler)
Milk in cardboard cartons
Pizza

Potato crisps and frozen potato chips
Salad dressings
Tortillas, tortilla chips
Vegetable gum (also gum on stamps and envelopes)
Vegetable oil
Vegetable starch
Yogurts

MSG (monosodium glutamate)

Also known as:
Flavour enhancer
E621

WHERE WILL YOU FIND IT?

Chicken nuggets
Chinese foods
Crisps
Fish Fingers
Flavour enhancers
Flavoured noodles
Gravy and packet sauce
Hydrolysed vegetable protein and vegetable protein
Pork pies/sausages
Tinned, frozen and packet soup
Soya sauce
Stock and stock cubes
Tinned beans, sweetcorn and mushrooms
Vending machine drinks
Yeast extract (Marmite and Vegemite)

Kiwi

Kiwi is not yet classed as a major allergen although many people think that it should be.

Also known as:
Chinese gooseberry
Chinese egg gooseberry
Golden kiwi fruit
Kiwi paste – used as a fat replacer in bakery goods

Desserts
Fruit drinks
Fruit salads
Health drinks
Jam
Smoothies
Yogurt

Latex

People with latex allergy can have an anaphylactic reaction to a minute amount of latex left on a food which has been handled by someone wearing latex-rubber gloves, so it is much safer for anyone handling food to use non-latex gloves. People with latex allergy can also react to the following foods:

Avocado
Banana
Chestnut
Fig
Kiwi
Papaya
Peanut
Soya

Nightshades

Although nightshade plants are not normally allergens, a small number of people react badly to them, especially to tomatoes and potatoes. Those who are allergic to chillies or peppers may also have a problem with chilli-based spices.

The nightshade family includes:
Aubergine
Bell Peppers/sweet peppers (red, green, yellow, Romano)
Cayenne Pepper
Chilli pepper and peppers
Hungarian Pepper
Paprika
Pimiento
Potatoes
Tabasco
Tobacco
Tomatoes

NB: Black and green peppercorns are not part of the nightshade family.

Sugar

Increasingly, sugar is being seen as a problem so many people are looking to at least reduce their consumption.

Many companies are replacing sugar with alternative sweeteners such as maltitol. These may be low calorie but are not much lower than sugar on the glycaemic index and often cause digestive upsets.

On labels, 'sugar-free' means that the product does not contain actual sugar, not that it is free of alternative natural or man-made sweeteners, so you need to read the label carefully. You will also now come across the term 'free sugars'. These sugars are naturally present in honey, syrups and fruit juices. They are different to sugar found naturally in foods such as lactose – the milk sugar found naturally in milk products – or fructose, the fruit sugar found naturally in whole fruits.

Natural, relatively unprocessed sugars/sweeteners alternatives

Also known as:
Agave (unprocessed)
Fruit sugar
Honey
Maple Syrup
Molasses and Treacle
Stevia (pure)

Processed sugars or sugar syrups

Also known as:
Invert Syrup
Corn syrup
Dextrose
Fructose
Glucose/Glucose Syrup
Golden Syrup
High Fructose Corn Syrup (HFCS)
Invert Syrup
Malt Syrup
Maltose
Sorbitol
Sucralose
Sucrose
Xylitol

Artificial or non sugar-derived sweeteners:

Acesulfame Potassium
Artificial sweetener
Aspartame
Saccharin

WHERE CAN YOU FIND THEM?

Almost any ready-made or manufactured foods or drinks

5
Allergy risk areas

There are six main areas where a restaurant or café serving allergic customers need to know what they are doing or they can get into trouble.

1. Prebooking information

2. Menu design

3. Recipe design

4. Front of house

5. Ordering and storing food

6. Preparing and cooking food

PREBOOKING INFORMATION

The vast majority of free-from 'eaters-out' will check out an eaterie online before they visit it. So, your online presence, be it a website, Facebook page or some other online presence, is extremely important.

There is a lot of competition out there these days so your site must look appealing but be easy to navigate. If potential customers cannot find the information they want easily, they will leave the site and not visit your eaterie.

You need to give clear and comprehensive information about what you are offering and what you do to keep your free-from customers safe. (If you use separate fryers for gluten free fish or chips, or separate toasters for gluten free toast, say so.)

This may be a chore to set up but a clear and comprehensive site will give potential customers confidence that you understand about catering for allergic, coeliac and free-from customers and that you know what you are doing.

Describe some of your free-from dishes and make them sound appealing.

Provide potential customers with an easy way to contact you – an email address or a telephone number. Many food sensitive people, especially if they have potentially fatal allergies, will want to talk to the eaterie they are planning to visit and nothing will put them off more than not being able to contact you easily.

If they do contact you, be polite, understanding and, above all, patient. You may know that you do things properly, but they do not and it is their life that could be at stake.

Surveys suggest that the most important element in ensuring a return visit by a free-from or allergic customer is not the quality of the food but the service they received. Setting up a good relationship from the start is crucial in this.

MENU DESIGN

If your customer has not checked your establishment out online or spoken to you on the phone, then you have to establish that relationship with them as soon as they arrive. Gaining your allergic customer's trust is the most important thing you can do, and your menu is crucial in doing that.

By law, you must use clear signposting to direct the customer to where they can find information about any of the 14 major allergens in your food. This would normally be a prominent notice on your menu or in an obvious place in your establishment. It should tell allergic customers that you can provide them with accurate information about any allergens in your dishes. This will also raise awareness of allergy among your other customers and remind your staff to be aware of the needs of allergic customers.

Whether you choose to have separate 'free-from' menus, or to incorporate the information into your main menu, make sure that it is clear and comprehensive.

When describing dishes, make sure that descriptions of the dishes reflect their potential allergenicity e.g. satay sauce with peanuts; traditional Bakewell tart with almonds and egg.

However, do not specify allergenic ingredients in some dishes but not in others; the customer may think that because none are specified there are none in that dish.

In self-service restaurants in particular, make sure that all dish descriptions include any allergy information.

'Free-from' logos can be confusing as customers may not be sure whether they indicate the presence or absence of an allergen. It is less confusing if you just list the ingredients so that customers can judge for themselves.

When updating your menus always remember to update your allergen information.

RECIPE DESIGN

When designing recipes, include naturally free-from ingredients. You will be surprised how often you can use a naturally free-from alternative – cornflour instead of wheat flour as a thickener; coconut oil or olive oil instead of butter to fry with. Look at existing or traditional recipes; they may only use quite small quantities of specific allergens and it would be quite easy to substitute them.

When inventing a new recipe ensure that it does not include a small amount of an allergen (dairy, gluten, nuts…) that is not essential to the recipe. If the allergen can be left out it will increase the choice for allergic customers.

- Design recipes in layers or stages so that you can change different elements of the recipe according to who you are cooking for.

- When designing recipes be adventurous. Look at ethnic foods, for example, many of which never use dairy or wheat.

- Do not always try to create a free-from look-alike of an existing dish; sometimes this will work but sometimes it will not, so be open-minded and experiment with new ingredients.

- Remember that some allergens may have been used in ingredients from your suppliers such as celery in a stock cube, so always check ingredients carefully.

- If you use bought-in ingredients, check each batch to make sure that the allergens included have not changed; if they have, remember to alert all staff.

MAY I
INTRODUCE
OUR ALLERGY
AWARE
WAITER, SIR

FRONT OF HOUSE

Dealing with the customer:

◎ Every outlet should a have a minimum of two staff trained in allergy management so that one is always available.

◎ Include basic allergy training in the training of all your staff.

◎ Be pro-active – but not pushy. Offer to call the allergy-aware staff member if the customer would like more information.

◎ Remember that although you know your processes and how safe they are, your customer does not and it is their life that could be at stake so always be patient and explain fully the measures that you take to keep them safe.

◎ If the wait-person does not understand what the customer is asking, or does not know the answer, it is very important that they do not pretend to understand or guess the answer. They should politely tell the customer that they do not understand, or that they do not know and will try and find out. If they refer the query to the kitchen and the kitchen staff do not know, they must tell the customer that no one knows the answer.

Service and self-service – golden rules:

◎ Serve allergic customers separately.

◎ Never use the same serving implements to serve allergen-free and allergen-containing food.

- Never offer a dessert trolley to an allergic customer as the risk of allergic ingredients (nuts, cream, wheat and butter) migrating from one dish to another is very high.

- Lay out free-from dishes on a separate self-service counter to minimise the risk of a non-allergic dish being contaminated by allergic ingredients (like peanuts, cream, sesame seeds) from another dish.

- Ensure that every dish has its own allergen-free serving spoons to minimise the chances of contamination.

- Ensure that every dish that contains an allergen is clearly labelled, highlighting any allergenic ingredients.

ORDERING AND STORING FOOD

Ordering:

- Insist on full ingredients lists and clear labelling on all products.

- Check all deliveries, keep copies of all labels and ingredient lists for products you buy in.

- Always check the ingredients of different brands as they may be different.

- Always check to ensure that a product has not changed and if it has, ensure you know which allergens it now contains.

Storing:

If possible, store allergens in a separate part of the store room/fridges/freezers.

- Store all 14 allergens (cereals containing gluten, milk, peanuts, tree nuts, sesame seeds, celery, eggs, fish, mustard, crustaceans, molluscs, lupin, soya, sulphur dioxide) in separate airtight containers to minimise the risk of contamination.

- Label containers clearly to avoid confusion. Ideally, have two different colours of container and colour code them into 'allergens' (red) and 'allergy free' (green).

- Always store allergen-free foods on shelves or in fridge/freezers above allergen containing ones, to avoid allergens dropping down onto allergen-free foods.

WHAT TO DO IF A CUSTOMER SUFFERS A SERIOUS ALLERGIC REACTION:

Have a list of allergy symptoms posted up in the servery:

◎ generalised flushing of the skin

◎ nettle rash (hives) anywhere on the body

◎ the customer is suffering with a sense of impending doom

◎ swelling of throat and mouth

◎ difficulty in swallowing or speaking

◎ alterations in heart rate

◎ severe asthma

◎ abdominal pain, nausea and vomiting

◎ sudden feeling of weakness (drop in blood pressure)

◎ collapse and unconsciousness

Not all these symptoms will necessarily be experienced. If the customer begins to suffer any of the above reactions, ask them if this has happened before? Ask them what happened next? Do they carry medication? Can they use it or
do they need help?

If you think a customer is having an allergic reaction, dial 999, call an ambulance immediately and tell the ambulance service that someone may be suffering a severe allergic reaction/anaphylaxis and that they may need resuscitation.

Have clear, detailed instructions as to how to get to, and get into, the eaterie easily available so that any member of staff can give detailed instructions to the ambulance. This is very important. If the ambulance is delayed it could be fatal.

While waiting for the ambulance, ensure that the customer does NOT try to walk around or to exert themselves. Do not leave them alone.

Send someone to wait outside the eaterie for the ambulance to speed their arrival.

PREPARING AND COOKING FOOD

Preparing food:

◎ If possible, prepare allergen-free dishes in a separate area of the kitchen from allergen containing ones.

◎ If this is not possible, ensure that everything used for the preparation of allergen-free foods (worktops, pans, implements, hands, plates, cutlery) has been thoroughly washed in hot, soapy water before the allergen-free food is touched.

◎ When preparing an allergen-free dish, think not only of the main ingredient but of subsidiary ones – like thickeners.

◎ If using ready-made ingredients like sauce, check their ingredients for unexpected allergens.

◎ If you run out of an ingredient like dairy-free spread for example, do not substitute another without checking its ingredients and telling the serving staff.

◎ Check every batch of bought-in dishes to ensure that the ingredients have not changed. If they have, alert staff and customers.

◎ When the allergen free dish is ready, store it in a separate part of the kitchen and label it clearly.

Cooking allergen free food:

◎ Use separate pans and implements (like wooden spoons, knives, spoons, forks) for cooking allergen free dishes. If you do not have separate pans, ensure that all pans and implements used for cooking allergen free dishes are thoroughly washed in hot soapy water and dried with clean towels (used towels could have specks of allergens stuck to them) before use.

◎ If possible, cook allergen free dishes immediately after the kitchen has been cleaned and before cooking allergy-containing ones, as this reduces the chances of contamination.

◎ Do not cook allergy-free dishes in the same oven as allergen containing dishes because of the risk of contamination. Or, if you are not able to use a separate oven, ensure that the allergen-free dish is cooked on the top shelf so as to avoid the chance of any allergen falling onto it from a dish above.

◎ Do not fry allergen-free foods in the same oil as allergen containing food. Specks of allergen may remain in the oil and contaminate the allergen-free food.

◎ Never just scrape off the allergenic ingredients like nuts or cream, from a dish and call it allergen-free. Residues of the allergen will remain on the dish and can cause a reaction.

6
Alternative ingredients and products

||||||||||||||||||||||||||||||||||||||||||||||||||||||||||||||||||||||||||||||||||||||||||||||||||||||||||||||||||||||||||||||||||||

Although there are alternatives to most ingredients, some work better than others. For example, while it is easy to replace cow's milk with half a dozen alternatives, most egg replacers work less well.

With some ingredients (cow's or goat/sheep milk or butter) you can just do a straight swop, with others (many of the alternative flours) you may need to adjust the amount of liquid in the recipe, or the cooking times.

Some other alternatives (coconut milk for cow's milk, for example) work very well but will change the flavour of the dish quite markedly – and sometimes for the better!

◎ Always experiment with a new ingredient until you get the hang of how it behaves and reacts.

◎ If you are only going to use an ingredient occasionally, store it in a freezer so that it remains fresh.

For lots of award winning gluten, dairy, nut, soya and other allergen free ingredients see the winners' pages on the FreeFrom Food Awards site, freefromfoodawards.co.uk

Cow's milk products and lactose-free alternatives

Goat, sheep and buffalo products are now quite easy to obtain and processed in modern hygienic dairies, are mild and pleasant, but, they are expensive. Because of their high fat content, goat, sheep and buffalo creams whisk well and can be used in most desserts, milk shakes, ice cream – and cappuccino!

Plant and nut

Soya milk

This has been a staple vegetarian ingredient for many years so there are many different varieties, both fresh and UHT.

Soya milk comes sweetened and unsweetened, flavoured and plain, fortified and unfortified. Most cook up well in sauces and soups and can be used for cappuccino, but some can separate in hot tea or coffee. Soya cream works as pouring cream, but you cannot whip it. Soya yogurts, both plain and fruit flavoured, are now

very good and can be used as an ingredient in a dessert, or as a dessert in their own right.

Hard soya cheeses are not unpleasant although they do not bear much resemblance to real cheese. Soya cream cheese is more successful. You can also get soya cheese slices which melt reasonably well for topping pizzas or burgers.

Oat, nut and rice milks

There are now a wide variety of other plant, grain and nut milks, all of which are pleasant enough on cereals and many of which can be used for cooking. Oat milk is good for soups and sauces (but be aware that not all oat milks are gluten free); rice milk is quite thin and sweet and is best in desserts; nut milks are pleasant but some taste quite strongly of nut.

Coconut milk and oil

Coconut milk is an excellent cooking milk to which very few people react, but it has a very distinct flavour. It is extensively used in Southeast Asian cooking. It comes in tins and can be used, well stirred, directly from the tin. It also comes in cartons. Cold pressed coconut oil from sustainable sources is an excellent butter substitute and works particularly well in rich sauces to which it gives a rich, smooth texture. However, compared with cow's milk, it is expensive, as is coconut yogurt.

Dairy-free spreads

There are several dairy-free spreads on the market but check the ingredients carefully as many spreads which may appear to be dairy-free – such as olive oil spreads – actually contain whey or casein. Most spreads are flavourless and harmless and can be used in sauces and baking (for example in pastry and cakes). They are not good for frying food in – use olive oil instead. Avoid spreads using hydrogenated fats if at all possible.

Egg alternatives

Egg-based dishes

From 2017, the Australian company, Orgran, have made an 'Easy Egg' product (winner of the 2018 FreeFrom Food awards) based on chickpea flour which makes remarkably good scrambled eggs, omelettes and frittata. However, it is not intended for baking. There are a number of egg replacements available for baking, most of them soya-based, but none have the lifting, setting or emulsifying qualities of eggs.

However, some vegan recipes use chickpea/gram flour that works surprisingly well, even for making meringues. Search for recipes online.

Cakes and baked goods

Raising agents (like baking powder, bicarbonate of soda, cream of tartar, glucono delta lactone) can be substituted in cakes or baked goods where the egg only plays a lifting or setting role, for example, any cake which has plenty of other textures or flavours. The cake will not be as light, but quite acceptable, especially if it includes fruit.

Raising agents do not work as well in baked goods without eggs, (such as a simple sponge cake) where the egg plays not only a lifting and setting role but provides texture and flavour. If you need to make egg-free sponges, there are a few brands of gluten/wheat/egg free mixes which make quite reasonable sponge cakes.

Custards and creams

Cornflour and arrowroot can be used to make creams and custards as long as care is taken that they do not become too claggy or floury. They will also be better if well-flavoured.

Mayonnaise

There are a number of good brands of egg-free mayonnaise.

Pancakes and batters

Pancake batter can be made very successfully without eggs. Just use the relevant flour with water or an allergen free milk. Batters will not hold together as well as if they were made with egg but are still viable.

Pasta

Use any of the dozens of egg-free, fresh or dried pastas on the market.

Gluten and wheat alternatives

Gluten, in the guise of wheat and wheat flours, starches and thickeners, is widely used within the food industry both as an ingredient and in the manufacture of ingredients.

This means that great care must be taken when using anything which is not a primary ingredient. Check the ingredients list on the packaging.

NON-WHEAT FLOURS

Gluten-free bread flours include combinations of buckwheat, gram (chickpea), corn/maize, millet, potato, rice and tapioca flour.

These are not easy to use as they lack the elasticity and setting quality of gluten. As a result, bread may rise (thanks to yeast or raising agents) but promptly fall again to produce brick-like loaves.

It is now possible to buy xanthan gum, which, if added in moderation, makes a reasonable substitute for gluten, although some people also have a problem with xanthan gum.

If you do wish to experiment with alternative flours here are a few notes on their properties for which we are grateful to Andrew Whitley. (Andrew, founder of The Village Bakery, gives courses on craft and gluten free baking in Scotland – see BreadMatters.com.)

Buckwheat flour

Very little binding power and a strong flavour which some people love. Widely used in Russia to make porridge and pancakes (blini). Use in combination with other flours.

Chestnut flour

Good binding properties and very distinctive, sweet flavour which may be overpowering. Good in combination with other flours. Expensive.

Cornflour/starch and corn/maize meal

Cornflour is the purified starch of the maize meal. A good, cheap thickener with good binding properties and useful in combination with other flours in baking – too fine and tasteless on its own. Corn/maize meal is the whole maize seed ground into flour. Quite coarse and because it oxidises quickly, often leaves a bitter taste. Maize flour is the very finely ground maize meal from which all-bran and germ have been removed so it does not oxidise.

Gram/chickpea flour

High in protein, so good for binding. It is widely used for making flat breads in India. However, used on its own, gram flour can taste very beany and have a rather claggy, beany feeling in the mouth. Use in combination with other finer flours such as rice, potato or tapioca.

Lupin flour

Made from the seeds of the sweet lupin which has been bred to remove the bitter alkaloids. Very nutritious and with good binding qualities but strong flavoured. More importantly, 70 per cent of people allergic to peanut are also allergic to lupin so it is a dangerous flour to use when cooking for people with food allergies or intolerances.

Millet flour

A fine, bland flour. It goes rancid very quickly making everything taste bitter so needs to be bought from a source with a quick turnover and kept in the freezer. Works best in combination with a strong flour like gram flour.

Potato flour/starch

The flour is the dried and ground potato tuber; the starch is a refined derivative of potatoes. In moderation (not more than 20 per cent) both flour and starch can give some binding and lightness but more than 20 per cent will become gummy and heavy. Very little flavour but good as a thickener.

Quinoa flour

Light, creamy flour from the seeds of the quinoa plant from South America. Not much binding power as a flour and a distinctive, slightly bitter taste, but very nutritious.

If you cook the grains like rice until they have absorbed as much water as they can then beat them to a sticky mush, they will aid binding and moisture retention, but do not use more than 10 per cent of the mush in the dough. Not widely available so expensive.

Rice flour – brown and white

Neither white nor brown rice flour have much binding power but are useful in combination with other stronger flours like gram or maize. Even when finely ground, rice flour can have a gritty texture when baked, and can leave a slightly bitter taste. Ground rice (much coarser) can also be used for cakes in much the same way as polenta.

Soya flour

Although excellent nutritionally, (high protein mainly. But since it is used in such small quantities it is not really that relevant) soya flour, if used at more than 5 per cent of the total weight, gives a very heavy texture and an unpleasant taste to the product. Because of its high protein levels, it can have an egg substitute effect in cakes and biscuits (most egg replacers are based on soya) but this does not outweigh its disadvantages.

Tapioca flour

Ground from cassava roots. Very light and bland but a reasonable binding quality. In moderate amounts gives a pleasant chewy texture to breads. If it forms more than 50 per cent of the flour in bread or pastry, the texture can become dusty and strange background flavours emerge. Use at 5 per cent to 10 per cent in bread and up to 40 per cent in pastry or biscuits.

Bread and breakfast goods

Over the last few years a number of companies have produced very acceptable part baked, frozen or long life breads, rolls, baguettes and croissants. These taste reasonable (if not always brilliant) and look like the original.

Crackers

There are many good gluten-free crackers now on the market.

Biscuits, cakes and other baked goods

There are of course many prepared products on the market, but making good gluten free cakes and biscuits is far easier than making bread, especially if you are using eggs.

The proprietary gluten free flours on the market work quite well, especially if you add a little xanthan gum. Alternatively, combinations of the stronger flours (gram or maize) with the finer, lighter flours (white rice, potato, cornflour/starch or tapioca), in approximately equal quantities, gives a reasonable balance which holds together well without being too strongly flavoured. They are very successful in cakes, although biscuits can be a bit crumbly.

You can also use ground gluten-free oats (rolled oats whizzed for some minutes in a food processor) in combination with some of the finer flours. Oats give quite a coarse, slightly crumbly texture, but lots of flavour – excellent for hearty cake such as gingerbread.

Breadcrumbs

If you have made/bought gluten free bread you can merely crumb your bread. If not, you can buy proprietary gluten free breadcrumbs which work quite satisfactorily.

Pastry

Combination flours for cakes and biscuits work best. Use 60 per cent gram to 40 per cent rice, made in the normal way, gives a well textured, quite crisp and flavoursome pastry although it is very crumbly. Adding a small amount of xanthan gum helps hold it together. To make it milk free as well, just use a dairy free spread or vegetable fat. However, it is now possible to buy readymade gluten-free pastry which can be kept in the freezer.

Pasta and pizza bases

There are a number of excellent dried, and now fresh, gluten free pastas and pizza bases on the market, based on everything from corn to mung beans.

Sausages

Although traditionally most UK sausages use a substantial amount of wheat-based rusk, sausages using gluten free rusk and fillers, or just pure meat, are now widely available. Alternatively, use (or make) pure meat sausages which use no fillers at all. Frankfurters, chorizo and other continental sausages may be free of gluten but check ingredients carefully, especially for milk products.

Sauces and thickeners

Cornflour/starch, potato flour and arrowroot all work well as thickeners for sauces, both savoury and sweet. Use as flour but be aware that you will need approximately 30 per cent less by weight of these starches to thicken the same volume of liquid.

Beer

You can now buy excellent gluten free beer, lager and stout.

Nuts and peanut alternatives

There are fortunately, relatively few mainstream dishes that depend on tree nuts or peanuts as their main ingredients.

Nut allergies can be very difficult to cope with because peanuts, in particular, can be used as a cheap substitute ingredient for other more expensive ingredients such as almonds. However, they present far fewer problems for the chef than, for example, gluten.

Seeds as alternatives

In most dishes where nuts are used for decoration or for additional flavour, including most vegetarian dishes, you will be able to substitute sunflower seeds or pumpkin seeds. They have a similar nutritional profile (starch and protein contents) and have an excellent flavour, especially if toasted or roasted before use.

Pesto

Pine nuts are a seed, not a nut, so should not normally pose a problem for those allergic to either tree nuts or peanuts. However, some people do also have a problem with pine nuts.

Since pine nuts are expensive there is always a risk that they might have been at least part substituted by peanuts so always check pesto ingredients unless you make it yourself. Both sunflower and pumpkin seeds make excellent pesto, either with basil or with another fresh herb such as coriander.

NB: Remember to note and list any herbs that you use as although they are not 'major allergens', some people are allergic to a number of herbs. Common herb allergies include anis, coriander, cumin, fennel, parsley, artichoke, and hibiscus.

Satay sauce

Provided your allergic customer can eat tree nuts you an make a very good satay sauce with cashew nuts; alternatively, use sunflower or pumpkin seeds.

Peanut butter

There are now a couple of peanut free 'peanut butters' on the market which taste remarkably like the real thing. Typically, they can include seeds instead of peanuts, like pumpkin seeds, sunflower seeds and brown linseeds.

Marzipan

You can make marzipan from ground rice or semolina, but neither are very satisfactory. However, almonds are one of the least allergenic of the tree nuts and some people who cannot tolerate Brazil nuts, walnuts, hazelnuts or cashew nuts can tolerate almonds.

Sugar alternatives

Many people who want to avoid sugar may not want to consume artificial sweeteners. So for the occasions when a sweetener of some kind is needed, there are a number of natural alternatives to refined white sugar.

Natural syrups (like maple, brown rice, coconut, fruit, agave) have excellent, if strong, flavours and can be used as an alternative to sugar – although they will do little to reduce the overall sugar content. They can usually be found in health food stores.

Fresh or dried fruit are ideal sweeteners, especially for people who are diabetic, as they are high in fibre, so slow to release their sugar content. Puréed, both work very well in desserts and cakes.

Fruit concentrates also work well. Although the sugar content is higher than whole fruit, the texture can be easier to incorporate into existing recipes.

It is also interesting to note that flavours become much deeper and more concentrated when fruit alone is used as a sweetener, so it is worth experimenting with existing recipes, exchanging a fruit or concentrate for sugar. Even a raw cane muscovado as an alternative to a standard caster or granulated sugar, can improve both flavour and nutritional profile.

Conclusion

We do hope that we have now convinced you that catering for allergy and coeliac sufferers, and free-from-ers, is really not that difficult and can be very rewarding.

However, there may be many other things that you would like to know, so feedback on the manual is very welcome – please email me at michelle@foodsmatter.com with any suggestions, and we will try to incorporate ideas into future updates.

Happy catering!

Useful resources

Suppliers:

For award winning products and suppliers see the winners pages of the FreeFrom Food Awards

Recipes:

For over 1000 delicious gluten and dairy free recipes, many of which are free of most of the 14 major allergens, see foodsmatter.com/freefrom_recipes/index.

Accreditations:

The charity **Coeliac UK** offer their prestigious gluten-free accreditation symbol to outlets that offer safe gluten-free food. Learn more here.

Allergen Accreditation – provides a framework for operators to develop their systems and procedures for managing the new legislation with a nationally recognised accreditation that they are allergy aware. allergenaccreditation.co.uk

Technical guidance on the food allergy regulations:

Excellent advice from the **Food Standards Agency** food.gov.uk

Training courses for managing allergy in food service:

The Food Standards Agency has developed a very good interactive online training tool which is a good introduction to the subject. food.gov.uk

Other courses:

Allergy Action. Hazel Gowland has been developing food allergy training and delivering courses to a wide range of audiences since 1995. allergyaction.org

Bowthornes Ltd Half-day courses used as an introduction suitable for both food preparation and service staff. fionahornetraining.co.uk.

Chartered Institute of Environmental Health (CIEH) will be producing a new qualification in developing allergen awareness with a new classroom-based qualification: Level 2 Award in Food Allergen Awareness, and e-learning module: Serving the Allergic and Food Intolerant Customer.Food Allergy Awareness Training and Consultancy (FATC) FATC has been set up to educate and assist the catering industry to become Food Allergy Aware, as well as to support those affected by food allergies. cieh.org.

Food Allergy Awareness Training and Consultancy (FATC) FATC has been set up to educate and assist the catering industry to become Food Allergy Aware, as well as to support those affected by food allergies. fatc.co.uk

Gluten-free Training for Caterers. Online and face-to-face training from coeliac bakers who have run their own gluten, wheat and dairy-free bakery since 2005. glutenfreetraining.co.uk.

Glossary

||||||||||||||||||||||||||||||||||||||||||||||||||||||||||||||||||||||||||||||||||||||||||||||||||||||||||||||||||||||||||||

Adrenalin
a natural hormone, produced in the body as a stress response, which when administered intra-muscularly, can help support the body during anaphylaxis.

Allergen(ic)
(descriptive of) an ingredient which triggers an allergy or immune-related intolerance in people who are sensitised to the ingredient

Allergy
rapid, adverse, immune-triggered response to an allergen

Anaphylaxis
the most acute form of allergic reaction, involving extreme symptoms such as drop in blood pressure, swelling and wheezing, collapse, which can be life-threatening

Antihistamines
medicine used in the treatment of allergies and other reactions which involve the release of histamine in the body

Autoimmune response
self-attacking response of the immune system, leading to tissue damage; coeliac disease is caused by an autoimmune response to gluten

Coeliac disease
autoimmune disease caused by gluten in the diet, and affecting 1 per cent of the population

Crohn's disease
a severe inflammatory bowel disease, usually affecting the small intestine, characterised by pain, diarrhoea and under-nutrition; those with the condition may be intolerant to milk and other foods

Cross reaction
allergic reaction to an allergen which is similar in chemical structure to a different allergen to which the sufferer already reacts. For example, hay fever sufferers – who react to pollens – may react to food components which are similar to pollens. Birch tree pollen, for instance, can be cross-reactive with raw carrots and apples

Enzyme	a chemical which brings about a metabolic reaction, typically in relation to digestion; lack of the enzyme lactase in the body causes lactose intolerance
Fermentable Oligosaccharides, Disaccharides, Monosaccharides, & Polyols (FODMAP)	any one of this group of sugars and carbohydrates – such as fructose in fruit, or lactose in milk – which may cause digestive symptoms, especially in people who suffer with irritable bowel syndrome (IBS)
Food allergy	allergy caused by a food constituent, almost invariably a protein
Food intolerance	physiological, adverse and delayed reaction to a food or food component
Food hypersensitivity	an umbrella term – either a food intolerance, coeliac disease, food allergy or other reaction to a food or food component
Gluten	dominant protein in wheat, implicated in coeliac disease
Gliadin	the gluten fraction in wheat, toxic to sufferers of coeliac disease
Histamine	chemical released by the body in response to an allergic invader, causing localised inflammation, and which can be at least partially countered by taking anti-histamine medication
Irritable bowel syndrome (IBS)	functional bowel disorder, characterised by either constipation, or diarrhoea, or both, diagnosed when structural disease is absent; sufferers may benefit from a low-FODMAP diet
Non-coeliac gluten sensitivity (NCGS) Non-coeliac wheat sensitivity (NCWS)	name given to a condition with similar symptoms to coeliac disease, that may be triggered by gluten in patients without either a wheat allergy or coeliac disease. It remains controversial, as some suspect that FODMAPs, not gluten, are the real cause of symptoms.

Acronyms

CMPA: Cow's milk protein allergy

GFD: Gluten free diet

MSG: Monosodium glutamate

Printed in Great Britain
by Amazon